MW00718051

In dreams we see
the future.

Treasure your dreams:
they are your wealth.

The power of a dream
is not in having
it but in living it.

Like a star, even the smallest dreams shine bright.

nurture your childhood dreams
and they will become real
as you grow older.

Hope, courage, and strength
flourish in dreams.

SANDRA MAGSAMEN's pictures and verse capture the
simple pleasures and daily truths of life. Her work acknowledges,
and is inspired by, the people who fill each day, each hour, and
each moment of our lives. Magsamen founded Table Tiles, Inc.—
her decorative accessories and gift business—in 1991. Her unique,
hand-crafted work is sold throughout the world.

Pictures and verse by Sandra Magsamen
© 1999 Hanny Girl Productions, Inc.
Exclusive licensing agent Momentum Partners, Inc., NY, NY

S Editions is an imprint of SMITHMARK Publishers.

This edition published in 1999 by SMITHMARK Publishers, a division
of U.S. Media Holdings, Inc., 115 West 18th Street, New York, NY 10011

S Editions books are available for bulk purchase for sales promotion and premium use.
For details, write or call the manager of special sales, S Editions,
115 West 18th Street, New York, NY 10011; 212-519-1215.

Distributed in the U.S. by Stewart, Tabori & Chang, a division of
U.S. Media Holdings Inc., 115 West 18th Street, New York, NY 10011.

ISBN: 1-55670-898-X
Printed in Hong Kong

10 9 8 7 6 5 4 3 2 1